# Akathist
# to
# Saint Daniel the Hermit

Anna Skoubourdis
Nun Christina

**Published by: Virgin Mary of Australia and Oceania 2022 ©**
oceanitissa@gmail.com
www.oceanitissa.com.au
Youtube: Nun Christina Oceanitissa

Subscribe to receive updates and Orthodox Christian creative media

www.oceanitissa.com

## Troparion

## Tone 8

In thee, oh, Father, the one created in the image of God was saved, for taking up the Cross, thou didst follow Christ and, by thy deeds didst teach us to overlook the flesh, for it is perishable, but to be attentive to the soul since it is immortal. Therefore, oh, pious Father Daniil, your spirit rejoices with the angels.

## Akathist

### Kontakion 1

To the lover of prayer and ascetic life, to the wise guide on the path of salvation, to the one who is the praise of the hermits and the joy of the faithful, let us cry out with love: Rejoice, Holy Venerable Father Daniel, who always prayed to God!

### Ikos 1

The maker of angels and men called you to glorify the name of the Holy Trinity with your life as an angel in the flesh, and you, rejecting worldly care, made your life like a bright ray of the Sun of Justice, and, remembering your holy sufferings, with humility and joy, we say:
Rejoice, the honor of our ancestral Church;
Rejoice, for you showed yourself to be a lover of prayer since childhood;
Rejoice, for you have left your parental home for the hermit life;
Rejoice, for the hermit life has been your delight;
Rejoice, for you have loved the Lord more than you have loved your parents;
Rejoice, for you have always had them in your prayers;
Rejoice, for you brought your youth as a pure sacrifice to God;
Rejoice, pure face of humility;
Rejoice, the blossoming of the hermit virtues in your youthful body;
Rejoice, example of abstinence for young people;
Rejoice, beautiful praise of the elder;
Rejoice, for you strengthen us in good works through your prayers;
Rejoice, Holy Venerable Father Daniel, always praying to God!

### Kontakion 2

Although young, through a pure life and constant prayer, you acquired the wisdom of the elderly, with the gift of God, to Whom you sang incessantly: Alleluia!

**Ikos 2**

You have increased the untaken treasury of your pure faith with harsh toils, wanting more and more to share in the beauty of the life of an angel in the body, for which we lovingly say:
Rejoice, ever-watchful dove of the asceticism;
Rejoice, adornment of the monastic community;
Rejoice, for here you showed yourself as an example of perfect obedience;
Rejoice, the one who skillfully interwoven prayer with physical hardships;
Rejoice, most bright face of humility;
Rejoice, for you have brightened the night with your unceasing prayers;
Rejoice, famous praise of the ascetic monks;
Rejoice, flower of piety adorned by God;
Rejoice, for, living in a mortal body, you have become like the angels;
Rejoice, counselor of the spiritual life;
Rejoice, worker of the prayer of the heart;
Rejoice, for, through fasting and prayer, you resembled John the Baptist;
Rejoice, Holy Venerable Father Daniel, always praying to God!

**Kontakion 3**

As the buck desires the clean waters of the springs, so have you, Holy Venerable Father Daniel, desired the clear waters of the ascetic's toils, singing incessantly to God: Alleluia!

**Ikos 3**

Knowing the blessing of hermit places, you have carved your cell from a rock at Putna with the help of God-honoring people, increasing your efforts with wisdom, for which we bring you praises like these:
Rejoice, fragrant spiritual flower of the hermit life;
Rejoice, for you lived in much peace, strengthened on the rock of faith;
Rejoice, for the Holy Voivode Stephen often asked for your advice in the cell at Putna;

Rejoice, spiritual father of this glorious voivode of Moldavia;
Rejoice, for with deep wisdom, you have counseled him;
Rejoice, for you gave him the weapons of victory: fasting and prayer;
Rejoice, for you strengthened him in the love of God and country;
Rejoice, for he was strengthened spiritually through your prayers;
Rejoice, for you have dispelled the fog of doubt in his soul;
Rejoice, for you have assured him of victory over the enemies of our Orthodox faith;
Rejoice, for this great voivode obeyed you with humility and love in everything;
Rejoice, supplicant to God, together with Saint Voivode Stephen, for the glory of the Church and our nation;
Rejoice, Holy Venerable Father Daniel, always praying to God!

**Kontakion 4**

Knowing the love of Saint Voivode Stephen for God's house, you advised him to build holy places so that the faithful could always glorify God, singing to Him: Alleluia!

**Ikos 4**

A secret thought, inspired by God, led your steps to other monastic places, and starting from Putna, with the will of God, you stopped at Voroneţ, making your ascetic abode here, for which we bring you these praises :
Rejoice, for you have been very zealous towards ascetic toils;
Rejoice, for you were consulted by Saint Voivode Stephen here too;
Rejoice, for you received the multitudes of the faithful with love to your cell;
Rejoice, healer of spiritual and bodily sicknesses;
Rejoice, for you drove out the unclean spirits through your prayers;
Rejoice, you who cleanse the passions of our bodies;
Rejoice, chosen lily of the pleasant smell of the wilderness;
Rejoice, you who give much spiritual peace to those who pray to you;
Rejoice, you who strengthen the faithful in faith;
Rejoice, fulfiller of perfect love in Christ;
Rejoice, for, leaving the world, you have served it with your ceaseless prayers;

Rejoice, ascension of believers to salvation;
Rejoice, Holy Venerable Father Daniel, always praying to God!

**Kontakion 5**

Through you, Father Daniel, the words of the prophet who said, 'the desert shall rejoice, and blossom as the rose' came true, for the crowd of believers always surrounded you, singing together with you to God: Alleluia!

**Ikos 5**

Just as the candle is not placed in a vessel but in a candlestick to light those in the house, so you, fleeing in the desert, did not remain hidden, but through your teachings and your life, with the gift of God, illuminated the community of monks from Voroneţ, for which we bring you these praises:
Rejoice, kind father of Voroneț;
Rejoice, the wisest teacher of Gregorie, the Metropolitan of Moldavia;
Rejoice, skilled adviser of those shrouded by the whirlwind of temptations;
Rejoice, example of patience and humility;
Rejoice, bright torch lit in the candlestick of your heart cleansed of sins;
Rejoice, for you have shown yourself to be a pillar of prayer to your community;
Rejoice, for you have always learned the virtue of fair judgment;
Rejoice, highly skilled doctor of hidden thoughts;
Rejoice, for your teary prayers have become a preeminent spiritual sacrifice before God;
Rejoice, for you have gained great patience through fasting and prayer;
Rejoice, heavenly man;
Rejoice, earthly angel;
Rejoice, Holy Venerable Father Daniel, always praying to God!

**Kontakion 6**

You spent an angelic life on earth, making yourself an image and example to your disciples through prayers, long fasts, and vigils, you have become worthy to dwell in the land of the meek, Holy Father Daniel, the worshiper of God, the adornment of the hermits and the praise of the monks, who always sing: Alleluia!

**Ikos 6**

By purifying your heart, you acquired a lot of wisdom, guiding on the path of salvation all those who came to you full of the love of God, which is why we bring you these praises:
Rejoice, beloved spiritual father of Saint Stephen the Great;
Rejoice, worthy disciple of All-holy Leontius;
Rejoice, for you have followed this holy hierarch in ascetic toils;
Rejoice, for you have prayed together with Saint Leontius and Saint Voivode Stephen of Moldavia;
Rejoice, speaker with angels;
Rejoice, you who in your holy prayers showed yourself to be a very skilled theologian;
Rejoice, seer of God;
Rejoice, pure dwelling of the Holy Spirit;
Rejoice, for, being in a corruptible body, you tasted the sweetness of heaven;
Rejoice, for your prayers have become a ladder to heaven;
Rejoice, Holy Venerable Father Daniel, always praying to God!

**Kontakion 7**

Receiving wisdom from God, you humbly hid your holy toils, constantly instructing those entrusted to you for salvation to sing with love to God: Alleluia!

**Ikos 7**

Prayer being the plowing of the soul through which we cleanse our hearts towards repentance and the grace of God, you always had it on your lips and in your heart, for which we bring you these praises:
Rejoice, plower of pure prayer;
Rejoice, for by humbly praying, you have received God's grace;

Rejoice, for you have become like the angels through unceasing prayer;
Rejoice, for through prayer, as on a ladder, you have risen to spiritual things;
Rejoice, for you have brought salvation to the souls of those who lovingly consulted you through your prayers;
Rejoice, for you drove out the camps of demons through prayers;
Rejoice, for you have strengthened the faith of the wavering through your prayers;
Rejoice, for enemies have reconciled through your prayers;
Rejoice, for those who traveled with your prayers have returned to their homes in peace;
Rejoice, for you have always united prayer with the almsgiving;
Rejoice, for your prayers are welcome before God;
Rejoice, for the faithful are straightened through them in the grace received from God;
Rejoice, Holy Venerable Father Daniel, always praying to God!

**Kontakion 8**

Knowing that just as the body cannot live without air and food, so the soul cannot be alive and ascend to God without ceaseless prayer, you united the movement of your heart and your breath with it, singing ceaselessly to God: Alleluia!

**Ikos 8**

Your love of God has never alienated you from the love of the country in which God's name is truly glorified, and for that reason, we bring you these praises:
Rejoice, great lover of the house of God;
Rejoice, for the land of the country has been adorned with holy churches;
Rejoice, for Saint Stephen built them at your encouragement;
Rejoice, for the ancestral faith is strengthened through these holy churches;
Rejoice, for their beauty shows the beauty of the nation's faith;
Rejoice, for you have always taught that the right faith gives strength to the nation;

Rejoice, for the enemies of the country through the power of faith have been defeated;
Rejoice, for your ascetic cell was made a royal palace;
Rejoice, for, in the silence of your cell, Voivode Stephen, through your prayers, enlightened his mind and gained strength for victory;
Rejoice, for the door of your hermit's cell was always open, like that of your parental heart; Rejoice, for standing in prayer, in your cell, you were sweetened by the joys of heaven;
Rejoice, fulfiller of the beauty of the ascetic places of our nature;
Rejoice, Holy Venerable Father Daniel, always praying to God!

**Kontakion 9**

Your ascetic hardships amazed the angelic cohorts because with your unceasing prayers, self-restraint, and purity of heart, you resembled the angels with whom you sang unceasingly to God: Alleluia!

**Ikos 9**

Although you left the world to live away from its troubles, the multitude of believers followed you for their spiritual benefit through the gift of God, for which we bring you such praises:
Rejoice, Father, that you showed boundless love to those in need;
Rejoice, helper of the poor;
Rejoice, doctor of the sick by God's gift;
Rejoice, comforter of the afflicted;
Rejoice, all-wise adviser of young people;
Rejoice, strength of the elder;
Rejoice, benefactor of the orphans;
Rejoice, all-wise teacher of the mothers;
Rejoice, steadfast courage of the soldiers;
Rejoice, guide of purity;
Rejoice, joy of those who repent;
Rejoice, Holy Venerable Father Daniel, always praying to God!

**Kontakion 10**

The multitudes of believers, being convinced that God, through you, will listen to their prayers, seeing the fulfillment of the desires of those seeking God, sang to God together with you: Alleluia!

**Ikos 10**

Your life was blessed, being the spiritual son of Saint Hierarch Leontius of Rădăuţi, then the spiritual father of Metropolitan Grigorie Roşca, for which we bring you these praises:
Rejoice, good spiritual fruitfulness of Saint Leontius;
Rejoice, faithful follower of spiritual efforts;
Rejoice, you who have suffered with him in ascetic places;
Rejoice, for you have been with him spiritually all your life;
Rejoice, for, even after his death, you have remained inseparable from him in prayer;
Rejoice, for you have raised Hierach Grigory to the Church;
Rejoice, for you have guided him on the path of humility and wisdom, according to God;
Rejoice, you who were called to the priestly ministry;
Rejoice, for you have fled from it, considering yourself utterly unworthy;
Rejoice, for through this, an example of humility you have made yourself;
Rejoice, for, through your harsh hardships, you fully sacrificed yourself to God;
Rejoice, for, through your prayers and teachings, like a hierarch father, you guided all who came to you on the path of salvation;
Rejoice, Holy Venerable Father Daniel, always praying to God!

**Kontakion 11**

Your face painted next to that of Hierarch Grigorie, your spiritual son, shows the love and honor with which the great hierarch of Moldovia surrounded you, as well as the care you showed him, guiding him on the path of salvation and teaching him to always sing to God: Alleluia!

**Ikos 11**

Your face painted in the midst of the saints soon after you fell asleep shows your life of holiness known to all the righteous people, for which we bring you such praises:
Rejoice, spiritual father of the believers from Bukovina;
Rejoice, steadfast protector of Bukovina together with the Holy Great Martyr John the New of Suceava;
Rejoice, for you watch over us and bless us all who enter the sacred church from your holy icon;
Rejoice, for even after you fell asleep in the Lord, the crowds of believers ran to your grave;
Rejoice, for you have shared much consolation and strengthening in the true faith with the gift of God from your grave;
Rejoice, for we always feel the warmth of your love for God from your grave;
Rejoice, for your love as a father is testified by the stone of your tomb placed by your beloved spiritual son, Saint Stephen the Great;
Rejoice, for the stone slab of your tomb pours out secret warmth;
Rejoice, for your grave has always been guarded by the light of a candlestick;
Rejoice, for the flock of monks you shepherded always honored you as a father and saint;
Rejoice, for even now, you are advising us with your humble face;
Rejoice, the honor and adornment of the faithful;
Rejoice, Holy Venerable Father Daniel, always praying to God!

**Kontakion 12**

Through your face that watches over the door of the Voronet Monastery, you bless us with fatherly love, instructing us to sing with you to God: Alleluia!

**Ikos 12**

Eternal protector of Bukovina, all of us knowing you from our ancestors, Holy Reverend Father Daniel, praises like these we bring to you:
Rejoice, for your face as a father has been painted in the souls of the faithful with the indelible colors of Christian love;

Rejoice, for, having this image in their hearts, the Bukovinian faithful found comfort and strength in their times of hardship;
Rejoice, for the memory of your ascetic hardships is preserved and honored by our righteous people;
Rejoice, face of true monastic life;
Rejoice, you who united, according to God, the love of country and ancestral faith;
Rejoice, for the faithful always wanted to kiss your holy relics;
Rejoice, being in the grave, they have been the source of many healings to those who honor faithfully;
Rejoice, for the faithful always went with faith and love to Putna and Voronet, as you were a hermit there;
Rejoice, for today, all the people honor you together with Saint Leontius and Saint Stephen the Great;
Rejoice, for we celebrate the placement of your holy relics in the reliquary with unspeakable joy every year;
Rejoice, for this, by the will of God, was done for the spiritual benefit of Christian believers;
Rejoice, great praise of Bukovina;
Rejoice, trumpet that heralds the imperishable beauty of our ancestral faith;
Rejoice, Holy Venerable Father Daniel, always praying to God!

**Kontakion 13**

O Most Reverend Daniel, the praise of the Church of Bucovina, our spiritual father, of all those who worship God with true faith, deliver our country, monasteries, and churches with their holy ornaments from all danger and make us worthy to sing to God, together with you: Alleluia! (*This kontakion is repeated three times.*)

Repeat Ikos 1. Repeat Kontakion 1.

**Ikos 1**

The maker of angels and men called you to glorify the name of the Holy Trinity with your life as an angel in the flesh, and you, rejecting worldly care, made your life like a bright ray of the Sun of Justice, and, remembering your holy sufferings, with humility and joy, we

say:
Rejoice, the honor of our ancestral Church;
Rejoice, for you showed yourself to be a lover of prayer since childhood;
Rejoice, for you have left your parental home for the hermit life;
Rejoice, for the hermit life has been your delight;
Rejoice, for you have loved the Lord more than you have loved your parents;
Rejoice, for you have always had them in your prayers;
Rejoice, for you brought your youth as a pure sacrifice to God;
Rejoice, pure face of humility;
Rejoice, the blossoming of the hermit virtues in your youthful body;
Rejoice, example of abstinence for young people;
Rejoice, beautiful praise of the elder;
Rejoice, for you strengthen us in good works through your prayers;
Rejoice, Holy Venerable Father Daniel, always praying to God!

**Kontakion 1**

To the lover of prayer and ascetic life, to the wise guide on the path of salvation, to the one who is the praise of the hermits and the joy of the faithful, let us cry out with love: Rejoice, Holy Venerable Father Daniel, who always prayed to God!

Dismissal prayer.

## Biography

## December 18

The venerable Daniil was born in a village not far from Rădăuţi, to righteous parents, being baptised with the name of Demetrius. Having loved the spiritual life, when he was 16 years old, he left his parents' house and joined the community of the Rădăuţi Monastery dedicated to Saint Nicholas, growing in faith, good deeds, prayer and night vigils. Every day he read the writings of the Holy Fathers and the liturgical books, showing obedience and humbleness in everything he did by the abbot's decision. He became a monk as a reward for his efforts, by the name of David, but his aspiration for more severe spiritual efforts led him to the Saint Leontius of Rădăuţi Monastery, close to today's Laura village. There he worked together with the brethren of the monastic community by day and prayed unceasingly in his cell by night. Having seen his endeavours and noticing his continuous aspiration to God, the abbot of the monastery gave him the Great Schema, advised by his father confessor, receiving the name of Daniil.

Soon after he received the Great Schema he retired, with the blessing of his abbot, near Viţău brook, in the forests around Putna, where he dug a cell in a rock that can still be seen today, not far from Putna Monastery. His ascetic efforts would make him known rather soon, having been visited by many faithful who sought his advice and spiritual guidance, as well as his intercessions to God for the healing of their spiritual and physical ailments.

Of his many spiritual children that came to him rather often, one can mention the holy ruler Prince Stephan the Great (†1504), who received the spiritual advice and blessing of the pious hermit. Stephan is said to have come to the cell of the pious hermit for the first time in 1451 when his father was killed at

Reuseni. St. Daniil encouraged him and predicted that he would be the ruling prince, which came true after six years in 1457. Following his advice, the great Stephan founded Putna Monastery in 1466. After the monastery was consecrated in 1470, the pious hermit went to live at the Eagle's rock, near Voroneţ. Stephan the Great went to ask for his advice there too in 1476 after he was defeated at Războieni. The hermit encouraged him to gather his army again and defend the country and Christianity against the invading pagans. The prince followed his advice and promised that after every victory he would raise a church, and so he did. Thus, in addition to the great prince, Venerable Daniil was also protecting Moldavia through his continuous prayers well received by God. In 1488, Stephan the Great built Voroneţ Monastery in only four and a half months.

Then the venerable Daniil went to that community and was elected abbot. There, he advised the monastics and the neighboring hermits, having been spiritual father of many faithful who came to him for spiritual benefit. God also gave him the gift of miracles which the pious always try to hide. Yet, the healing of diseases and the casting out of evil spirits were signs of his holiness for which he was greatly venerated.

In 1496 St. Daniil fell asleep into the Lord, Whom he had served from his youth. The text on his gravestone laid by holy Prince Stephan reads: "This is the grave of our father David, hermit Daniil." In 1547, at the command of the metropolitan of Moldavia, Gregory Roşca (†1570), who had been a disciple of Venerable Daniil, his face was painted with a saint's halo over the entrance door, on the southern side of the church. The parchment St. Daniil holds in his hand reads: Come, my children, listen to me; I will teach you the fear of the LORD (Psalm 34:11).

On March 5, 1992, the Holy Synod of the Romanian Orthodox Church enlisted Venerable Daniil the Hermit in the calendar of saints to be celebrated on December 18.

Through his holy prayers, Lord Jesus Christ, our God, have mercy on us. Amen.

**Books published by Nun Christina Oceanitissa:**

The collective works of St Nektarios of Aegina.
The Philokalia 5: The full text in English.
The collective works of Elder Cleopa.
The Anacreontic Poems by Saint Sophronius Patriarch of Jerusalem.
The Life of Saint Paul of Thebes the First Hermit.
The Devil: The Cause of Sin by Saint John of Kronstadt.
Faith and the Orthodox Church by Saint John of Kronstadt.
The Monastic Rule of Saint Pachomius the Great.
Supplicatory Canon and Akathist to St Paisios.
Supplicatory Canon and Akathist to St Porphyrios.
Supplicatory Canon and Akathist to St George.
Supplicatory Canon and Akathist to St Anastasia.
Supplicatory Canon and Akathist to St Anna.
Supplicatory Canon and Akathist to St John the Russian.
Supplicatory Canon and Akathist to St Ephraim of Nea Makri.
Supplicatory Canon and Akathist to St John Maximovitch.
Supplicatory Canon and Akathist to St Dimitri.
Supplicatory Canon and Akathist to St Joseph the Hesycast.
Supplicatory Canon and Akathist to St Luke the Surgeon.
Supplicatory Canon and Akathist to St John the Baptist.
The Way of a Pilgrim.
Conversation with a Grieving Man by St Dimitri of Rostov.
The Inner Man by St Dimitri of Rostov.
Orthodox Prayer Book.
Daily Orthodox Prayer book.

www.ingramcontent.com/pod-product-compliance
Lightning Source LLC
LaVergne TN
LVHW010512160826
845677LV00012B/2812

* 9 7 9 8 8 4 6 3 5 0 1 6 8 *